Assessment

The suggested activities in the *Village life in India* materials will provide ample opportunities for teachers to undertake proper assessment of pupils' geographical progress. The activities have been designed to allow pupils to achieve levels 2–5 in the geography Attainment Target. These levels should describe the attainment of the overwhelming majority of pupils at Key Stage 2. There is no need for teachers to see assessment as something distinct from good teaching and learning. The identification of assessment opportunities, because they are directly related to learning objectives, is an integral part of, and support for, the effective planning of lessons. The activities provided in these materials have clear learning objectives. By making informal or formal decisions about whether pupils have achieved these objectives, teachers will be acquiring a range of assessment data. The challenge is to ensure that the gathering of assessment information is done in a way that is *manageable* and that the assessment information is *useful* to the teacher. Assessment outcomes not only provide the basis for reporting but should be used to give diagnostic feedback to pupils, and also to review the overall effectiveness of the curriculum.

Planning and assessment

Use the Level Descriptions in the geography Attainment Target to get a sense of appropriate learning outcomes for pupils of different abilities.

↓

Use the Programme of Study and the *Village life in India* materials to plan learning outcomes for the pupils' study of this distant locality.

↓

During learning, monitor achievement and form a judgement of how well pupils are performing in terms of the planned learning outcomes.

↙ ↘

Use assessment information to give pupils diagnostic feedback.

Use assessment information to review the overall effectiveness of the way the unit has been taught.

Studying distant localities

Stereotyping

Everyone will come to this study with their own set of ideas about what life is like in India. Teachers may want to start by finding out what pupils already think and know. Ask the pupils to make a list of the things that they would investigate if they were to visit this area themselves. What issues do they think they do not have enough information about? Who would they want to interview and why? What places would they want to visit? What scenes would they take photographs of?

To investigate the question of bias, pupils could collect 10 items which are important in their lives and which could be sent to Chembakolli to tell people about their own lives. Ask the pupils to imagine what people might think if they received these items. Might they believe, for example, that everyone in Britain wears Nike trainers, eats McDonalds and has a Game-boy? Would looking at these items in isolation create a biased impression of British life?

This activity could also be completed using about 30 photographs taken by individual pupils, which represent something important in their lives. The resulting photographs might show favouritism towards the pupil's pets, families or bedrooms.

RESOURCE SHEET 1

Resource sheet 1 can be used to encourage pupils to think more about India, and to present some of the information they may already know about this country. It is essentially a structured brainstorm which will enable teachers to assess the information pupils already possess before using these resources. It will also provide a reference which pupils can return to at the end of their study to compare their preconceptions with the information they have acquired.

Diversity

As the pupils embark on their study of Chembakolli it is important that they understand the huge diversity of Indian life. It is very easy to make the mistake of thinking that life in Chembakolli represents life in the whole of India. Pupils should recognise that this is only one locality. For them to believe that the rest of India is just like Chembakolli is as overgeneralised as believing that a village in Kent represents British life.

In order to give pupils a wider appreciation of Indian diversity, pages 37–47 of this book investigate general aspects of life in the Indian sub-continent: towns and cities, work, travel and links with other countries. This will enable pupils to place the locality of the Nilgiri Hills within a broader geographical context, make comparisons and draw conclusions which are not narrowly stereotypical.

Population, language and religion

Teachers may wish to introduce some more general information at the outset. India has a population of nearly 900 million people – about 16 times greater than Britain. Within this population there is a wide variety of life styles. In fact there is as much diversity across India as there is to be found in Europe. There are 15 national languages used across India. Hindi is the official language and English, an inheritance from the colonial period, is commonly used. Many people speak at least two languages.

India is a secular state. Its main religions are Hinduism and Islam, other religions being Sikhism, Buddhism and Christianity. Ask the pupils to use different information sources, such as library books or personal links, to investigate the different religions of India.

RESOURCE SHEET 2

Resource sheet 2 includes a bar chart which shows the percentage of Indian people belonging to different religious groups. Having analysed the information in the bar chart pupils can go on to make comparisons with their home locality. The Indian chart is based on percentages. Pupils will construct their chart based on actual numbers in their class. They need only make simple comparisons between the relative sizes of the bars in the two charts.

Village life in India

TEACHER'S BOOK

Steve Brace

Contents

CAMBRIDGE
UNIVERSITY PRESS

Introduction

● ●

Cambridge Primary Geography and the National Curriculum

Cambridge Primary Geography materials are designed to help teachers meet the demands of the revised National Curriculum and to provide the basis for exciting, challenging geography. *Village life in India* fulfils the requirement to study a locality outside the UK which contrasts with the pupils' home locality. It also allows pupils to study the themes of weather, settlement and environmental change within the actual context of their distant locality study.

Village life in India focuses on a locality in the Nilgiri Hills, based in the southern Indian state of Tamil Nadu. It updates and extends the ACTIONAID study pack on Chembakolli. While this new case study does not cover the whole of India, with its population of nearly 900 million people, it closely examines life in one particular area, which is then contextualised within a general overview of the Indian sub-continent. The Pupil's Book and Picture Pack will give children a secure knowledge of where the locality of the Nilgiri Hills is and what life is like for its inhabitants. Pupils will be able to investigate the physical and human features which give this place its geographical characteristics. They will see how these features affect life in this overseas locality and make comparisons between it and their home locality. They will also be introduced to the broader geographical context within which the locality is set and learn how it is linked to other places.

All of the materials embody the principle of enquiry, as required by the Programme of Study. Throughout, pupils are given opportunities to answer real geographical questions about places and geographical themes. The Pupil's Book is organised around a single overarching enquiry, namely: What is it like to live in an Indian village? Each chapter in the book is structured around a mini-investigation, expressed as a key question. Cumulatively, these mini-investigations, together with the use of the Picture Pack and Resource Sheets in the Teacher's Book, provide the knowledge and concepts pupils need to construct an answer to the overall enquiry question.

The materials enable teachers to deliver geography in accordance with OFSTED assumptions about good practice. The geography that is presented here encourages pupils to think analytically. At the same time, the materials are accessible because they focus on real localities and real people.

Climate

Climate will be dealt with in greater detail on pages 18–20 and Resource sheets 10 and 11. India has a great diversity of climatic conditions which include:

- the icy temperatures of the Himalayas, containing some of the largest expanses of snow and ice outside the polar regions;
- the hot season, between April and May, reaching over 35 °C;
- the rains of the monsoon, which in Cherrapunji, in north-east India – one of the wettest places in the world – reach 11,084 mm a year.

To understand the diversity of life in India, pupils should have the opportunity to compare images of Chembakolli with other images from around India. Picture cards 1 and 12 from the *Village life in India* Picture Pack will be useful here. They need to understand that this is a real place which has its own distinct characteristics. Pupils should also be helped to understand that the text and photographs in *Village life in India* only provide a certain amount of information and that they should consider what is 'around the edges of the photographs' and what information they do not have access to.

Geographical key questions

In examining distant localities it is important to use the same questions you would use to study the pupils' own locality. Using the geographical key questions (see below) will ensure pupils investigate the *geography* of this area. It will prevent them from concentrating on the exotic aspects of Indian life. For example, an over-emphasis on the clothes people wear or their religious observances provides only limited information about this area's geography.

Pupils should acquire an appreciation that, although they might live in circumstances very different to pupils in Britain, the people in this locality are real people who have families, homes and aspirations. Pupils need to recognise the features which make life different in this part of India from life in Britain. However, they should also have an understanding of the common links between their own lives and the lives of Indian people.

These geographical key questions will provide pupils with a geographical framework for their locality studies. They can be used to investigate the geography of any locality, be it in India, the pupils' home locality or a contrasting locality in Britain.

Geographical key questions
Who lives here and what do they do?
What is the climate like and how does it affect people's lives?
What is the physical environment like and how does it affect people's lives?
Is this place a rural or an urban location?
What are the buildings used for and what are they made from?
How do people travel around this place?
How is this place similar to or different from other places I have studied?
Which changes have occurred in this place, and which changes are going to take place in the future?
What links does this place have with other areas?

Name:

R1 Investigating life in India

Find a different person to answer each of these questions.
Write their name next to the number in the answer box and
write their answer in the box below their name.

What is the name of:

1 a type of food eaten in India;
2 a country which is near to India;
3 an animal which lives in India;
4 an Indian town or city;

5 a type of plant which grows in India;
6 an Indian religion?

1	4

2	5

3	6

Name:

R2 Diversity – religion

This bar chart shows how the population of India is divided between the different religions.

Religions in India

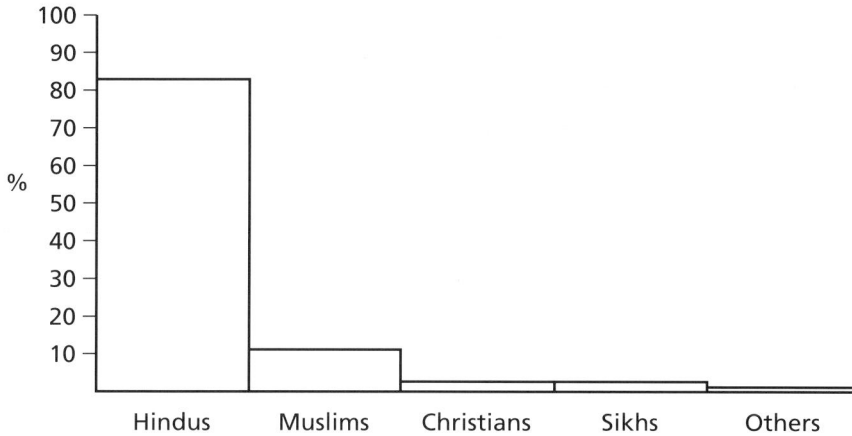

- Make a survey of your class to find out the numbers of pupils belonging to different religions. Record the results in the table.

religion	number

- Use the numbers in your table to make your own bar chart. Compare your chart to the chart showing religions in India. What differences or similarities can you see?

Religions in my class

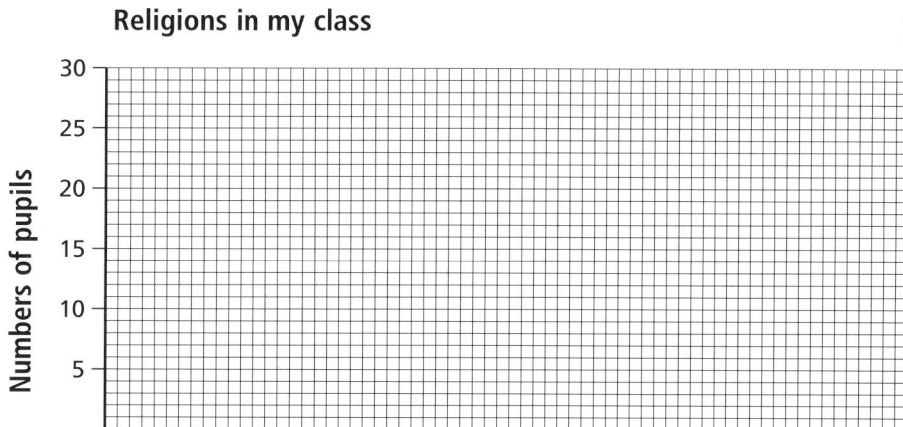

Geographical investigations

Throughout all their work on India pupils should be asking the questions:

- Where?
- How?
- Why?
- When?
- What if?

When planning geographical investigations it is useful to consider the geographical cube shown on the right. This approach brings together the key aspects of geographical skills, themes and places within the same work.

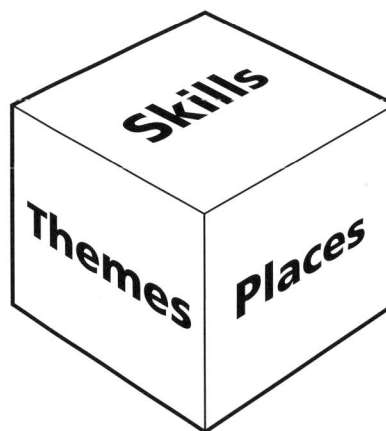

RESOURCE SHEET 3

Resource Sheet 3 is a geographical investigation sheet which allows pupils to identify the different aspects of their locality study by reinforcing the use of questions and evidence. It provides a reference for pupils to review which questions they asked about the place; the sources of information they used to find the answers to these questions and the answers they found. The final section of the sheet provides the chance for pupils to revisit their work and identify if there are any further questions they can now ask, building on the knowledge and understanding they have developed.

Teachers can also adapt the sheet so that pupils focus on particular themes such as landscape, jobs or homes. This approach could be used so that groups of pupils are asked to investigate different aspects of life in the area and then report their findings back to the rest of the class.

Similarities and differences

One of the key aspects of geographical enquiry is the investigation of similarities and differences between localities. The geographical key questions support this approach. By asking questions focused on geographical issues, pupils are required to provide evidence to support their answers.

If the pupils' school is located in an urban area it may be helpful to compare the Nilgiri Hills with the (rural) locality chosen as the contrasting UK locality. In this way pupils will be comparing rural Indian life with rural British life.

RESOURCE SHEET 4

Resource Sheet 4 shows how geographical investigations into similarities and differences can also be organised thematically. Pupils are asked to compare features such as landscape, weather, family life, homes, jobs, important places, journeys and transport and change. They could also suggest reasons for the differences.

RESOURCE SHEET 5

Resource Sheet 5 allows pupils to gauge their perception of a place by using a series of paired words. By plotting their responses they can produce a graph which can be compared to another graph showing their ideas about their own locality.

Name:

R3 Geographical investigation sheet

Investigating life in India

These are the questions I asked about the geography of Chembakolli and its neighbours:

I used these sources of information to answer the questions (e.g. photographs, statistics, books, video, computer):

These are the answers I found to my questions:

Other questions I can now ask about this area:

ACTIONAID

Name:

R4 Similarities and differences

Fill in the table to compare what life is like in the
Nilgiri Hills with your local area.

	The Nilgiri Hills	My local area
landscape		
weather		
family life		
homes		
jobs		
journeys and transport		
important places		
changes in the area		

Name:

R5 Quality of life

Place a cross on the line between each pair of words to show what you feel about the Nilgiri Hills. For example: if you think the people there are rich, put your cross near the word rich. If you think they are poor, put your cross near the word poor. You can put your cross anywhere between the two words depending on how rich or poor you think the people are. After you have completed each pair join all the crosses up to form a graph. Then complete a second graph for your local area. What are the differences between the two areas? Which area do you prefer and why?

Quality of life graph

interesting	boring	interesting	boring
quiet	noisy	quiet	noisy
modern	old	modern	old
friendly	unfriendly	friendly	unfriendly
clean	dirty	clean	dirty
rich	poor	rich	poor
spacious	crowded	spacious	crowded

name of area:

Nilgiri Hills

name of your area:

....

ACTIONAID

Mapping skills

At KS2 the geography Programme of Study requires that pupils should be taught to use geographical skills within the study of a locality so that they can:

- use appropriate geographical vocabulary;
- make plans and maps at a variety of scales, using symbols and keys;
- use and interpret globes, maps and plans at a variety of scales;
- use secondary sources of evidence – pictures, photographs and other sources to inform their studies.
- use IT to gain access to additional information sources and to assist in handling, classifying and presenting evidence.

It is essential that pupils develop a conceptual awareness of where places are. Throughout their localities work they should use maps of different scales. Pupils should be able to locate the Nilgiri Hills on a map of India and locate India on a globe or world map. Pupils ought to have the geographical understanding to recognise that Chembakolli is not, for example, located in northern India and India does not border France!

A CD-Rom is available to accompany this unit, entitled *Village life in India*, ISBN 0 521 57663 6. For further details contact 01223 325014.

RESOURCE SHEET

6
7
8

Three maps of different scales are provided in this resource book:

Resource sheet 6   India
Resource sheet 7   The Nilgiri Hills
Resource sheet 8   Chembakolli village

Each of the maps can be used for many different types of mapping skills activities, including:

• Types of map

Compare these three Indian maps with maps from Britain e.g. OS, A–Z or tourist maps. What are the differences? What different information do they show? Which maps are shown in plan or pictorial form? How are the maps laid out e.g. the patterns of settlements or the lines of communications? Pupils should compare maps of the same scale and compare the features shown on a map of a British village with those in Chembakolli.

• Direction

Pupils can identify directions on a map, at first using terms such as top, bottom, left or right. They should then move on to using the points of the compass. These terms should be used both when locating features e.g. Bangalore is to the south of Bombay, and also for example when planning journeys, e.g. for different people in Chembakolli village.

• Scale

Each map is of a different scale. Pupils should use the scale to identify the distances between different places and features. Information from the scale can be used in route planning.

• Key

Pupils should use the key on each of the maps to identify its main features. Where the key shows different land-uses it can be used to work out how much land is use for different purposes.

• Co-ordinates

Grid squares have not been drawn on the maps. However, teachers can add grids which are appropriate to their own pupils, e.g. large-letter number grids for younger pupils or smaller four-figure grid squares for older pupils. The co-ordinates can be used to locate different features on the maps.

Name:

Map of India

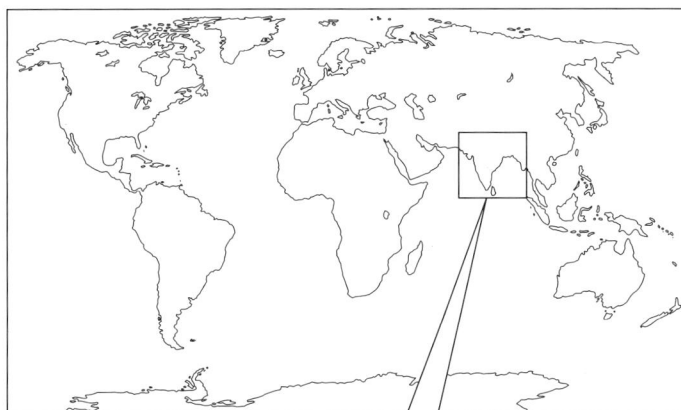

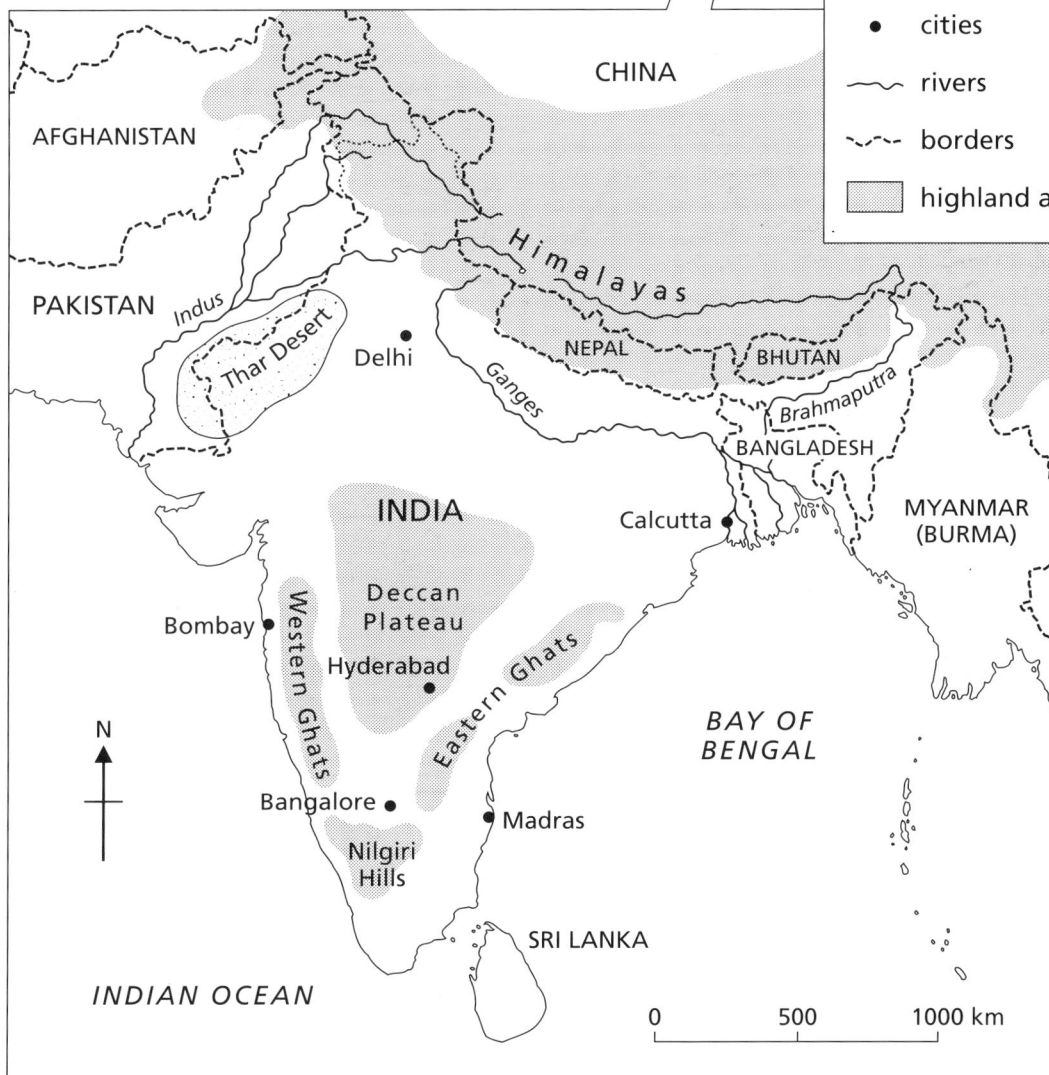

Key

- • cities
- ⌢ rivers
- –·– borders
- ▨ highland areas

CHINA

AFGHANISTAN

PAKISTAN

Indus

Thar Desert

Delhi

Ganges

NEPAL

BHUTAN

Himalayas

Brahmaputra

BANGLADESH

INDIA

Deccan
Plateau

Calcutta

MYANMAR
(BURMA)

Bombay

Western Ghats

Hyderabad

Eastern Ghats

N

Bangalore

Madras

BAY OF
BENGAL

Nilgiri
Hills

SRI LANKA

INDIAN OCEAN

0   500   1000 km

Name:

![R7] **Map of the Nilgiri Hills**

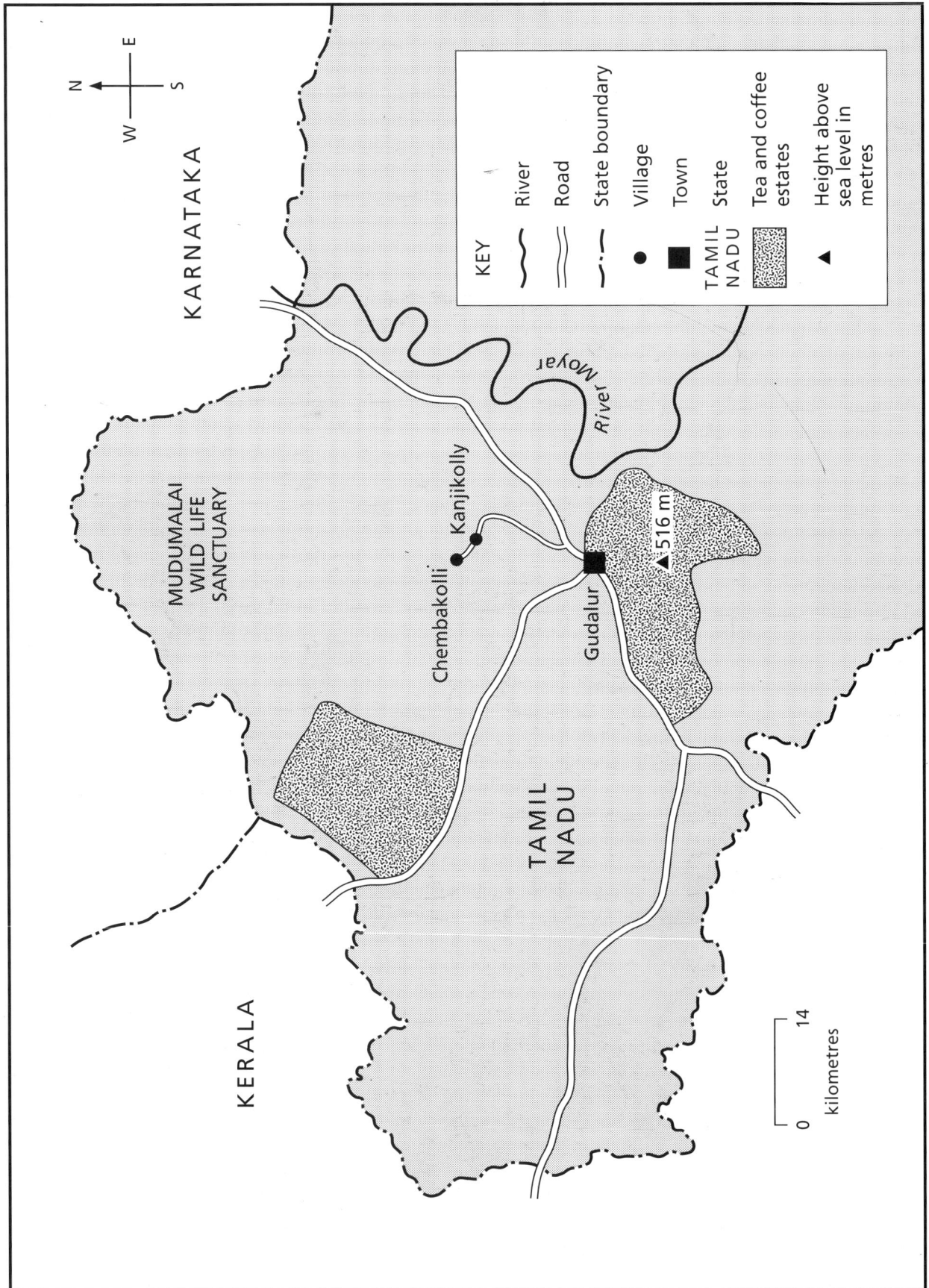

KEY

River	
Road	
State boundary	
●	Village
■	Town
TAMIL NADU	State
	Tea and coffee estates
▲	Height above sea level in metres

KARNATAKA

Moyar River

MUDUMALAI WILD LIFE SANCTUARY

Kanjikolly

Chembakolli

Gudalur

▲ 516 m

TAMIL NADU

KERALA

14 / 0 kilometres

Name:

Map of Chembakolli

R8

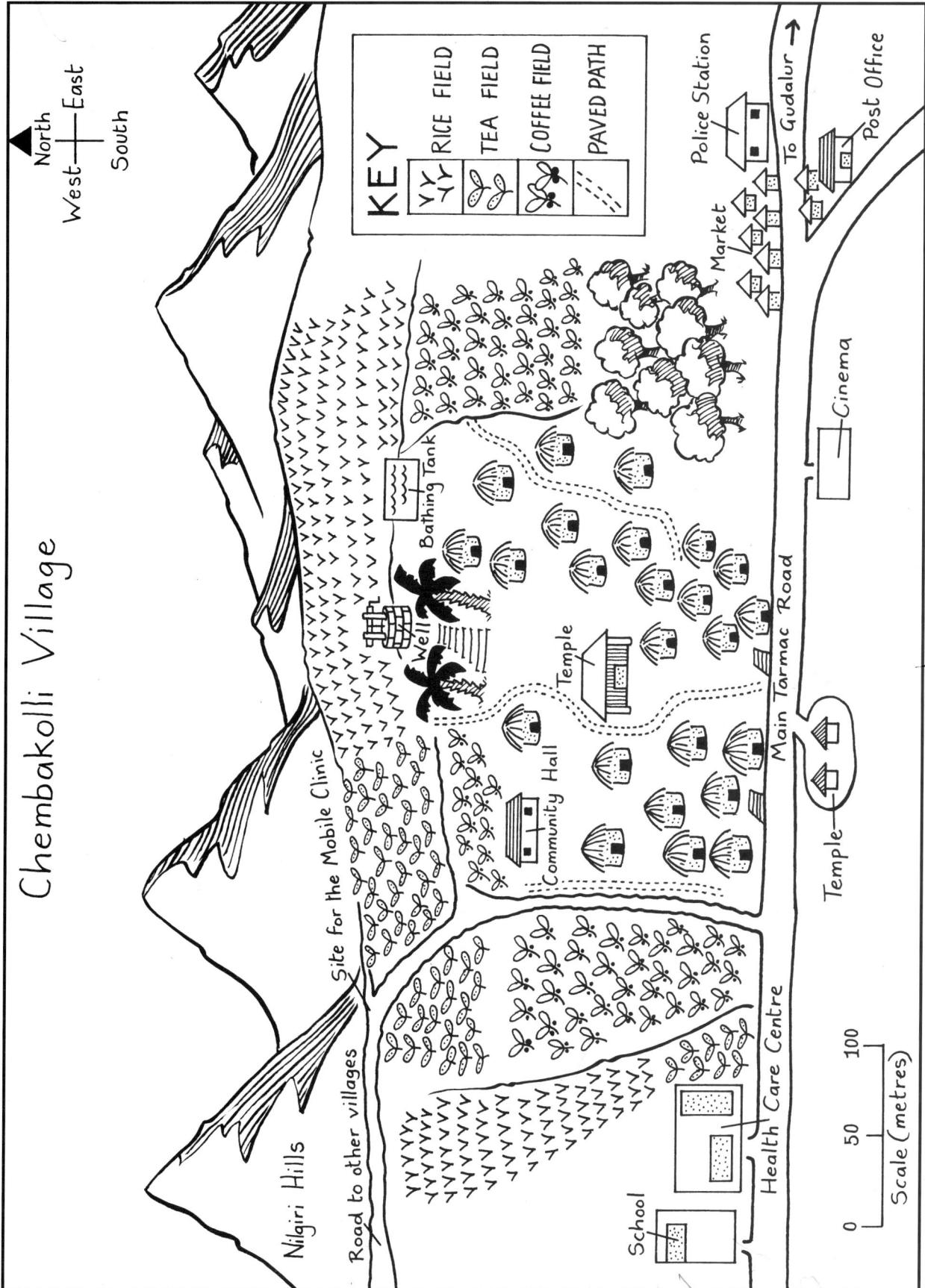

Chembakolli Village

North
West — East
South

KEY

| RICE FIELD | TEA FIELD | COFFEE FIELD | PAVED PATH |

Police Station
To Gudalur →
Post Office
Market
Cinema
Bathing Tank
Well
Temple
Main Tarmac Road
Community Hall
Site for the Mobile Clinic
Temple
Health Care Centre
School
Nilgiri Hills
Road to other villages

Scale (metres)
0   50   100

ACTIONAID

Storyboards and other language activities

Resource sheet 9 allows pupils to design their own film storyboard depicting different aspects of life in this area.

The pupils will need to plan a story with six sections; write a title for each section; draw the scene they would film and write a soundtrack to accompany each scene. Ideas for the storyboard could include:
● daily life in the Nilgiri Hills
● how life is improving in this area
● the Adivasi land rights demonstration.

Pupils can use the materials on *Village life in India* as stimulus for different language activities.

Ask the pupils to draw spider diagrams such as the one shown below of words related to different themes from this area. The words can then be used as the basis of a poem.

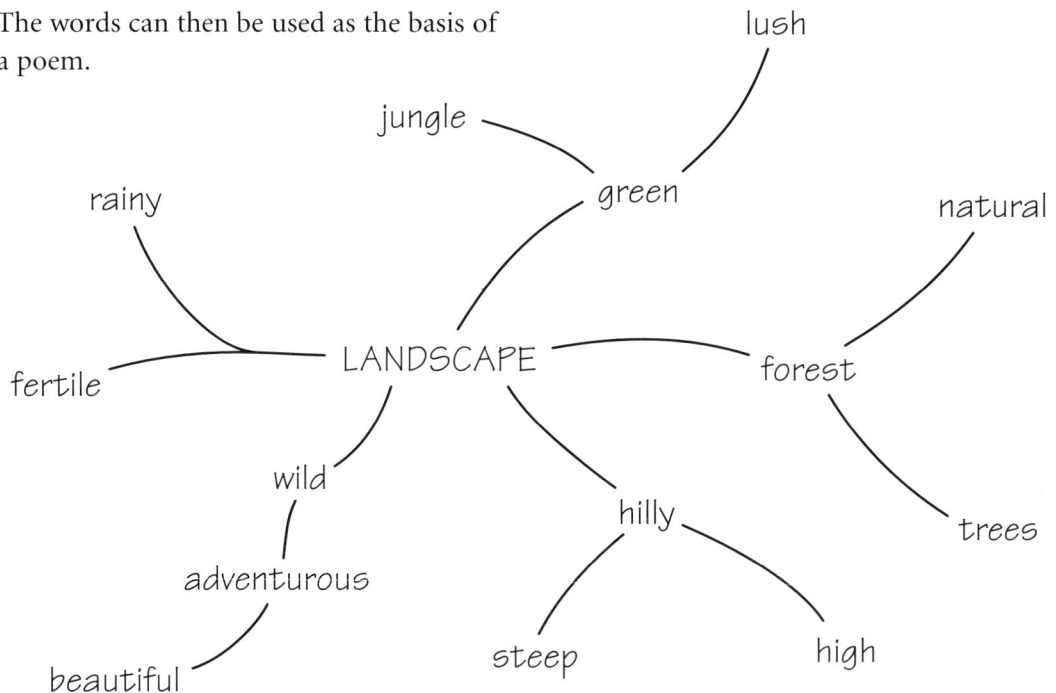

Pupils could also write 'adventure style' stories which will take the reader on different routes through the village. Ask the pupils to write these stories in the first person.

Write a visitors' guide to this area. Describe the main places of interest. What information would you need to know if you visited this area?

Use different words from the area as the basis for acrostics – poems where the first letters of each line form words.

Use a vocabulary bank of words from which the pupils choose to describe different scenes from this area.

lush

jungle

rainy   green   natural

fertile   LANDSCAPE   forest

wild

adventurous   hilly   trees

beautiful   steep   high

Pupils could write Haiku poems about the area using the three-line form of five syllables – seven syllables – five syllables. Here is an example:

Walking from the hills
As rain falls on forests green
To Chembakolli

Written by T. Ghazi

ACTIVITY As a review activity pupils can test each other through 'hot seating'. Write out a number of titles, such as families, journeys, weather, work, houses and change. In groups ask the pupils to select one card each. The pupils should then take it in turns to be in the 'hot seat' and answer questions from the rest of the group on their subject.

| **Name:**

R9 Storyboard

Use this storyboard to plan a film about India, divided
into six scenes. Draw a picture of each scene and give it
a title. Now, on a separate piece of paper, write a
description of what happens and what is said in each
scene.

1 Title:

2 Title:

3 Title:

4 Title:

5 Title:

6 Title:

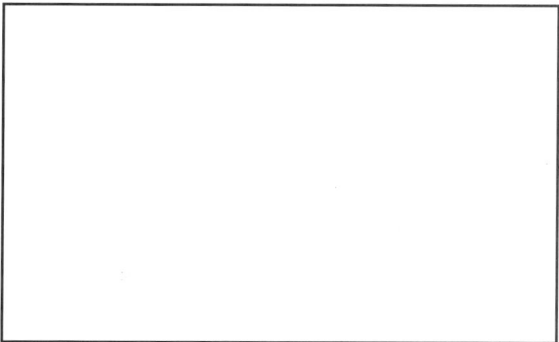

ACTIONAID

Location and climate

Chembakolli is in the Nilgiri Hills which are located in the Western Ghats, a range of mountains running down western India. This area of highland reaches up to about 2,500 metres above sea level and its vegetation spans tropical forest and scrubland.

The Nilgiri Hills are in the Indian state of Tamil Nadu. There are 25 states in India. Each state is divided into districts and each district divided into taluks. Chembakolli is located in Gudalur taluk.

This diagram shows the location of Chembakolli within India. Ask the pupils to draw a similar diagram for their own locality.

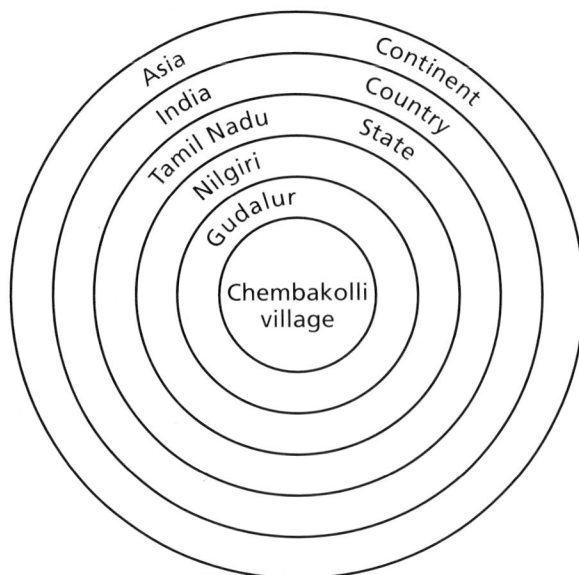

Climate in the Nilgiri Hills

Unlike Britain, with its four seasons of winter, spring, summer and autumn, this part of India has three seasons. This is a characteristic of the monsoon climate which is prevalent across much of India.

- Cool season: November to March
- Hot season: April to May
- Monsoon season: June to October

The data given in the climate graphs on Resource Sheet 10 is for Bangalore, the nearest city to the Nilgiri Hills. The temperature in Bangalore is slightly lower than many other places in India. This is because Bangalore is over 1,000 metres above sea level and the altitude lowers the temperature.

RESOURCE SHEET 10 11

By using Resource Sheet 10 and 11 pupils can draw their own climate graphs for this area and comparable graphs for London. This information is also included as an interactive graphic display on the *Village life in India* CD-Rom.

Pupils should discuss how the cycle of the monsoon affects people's lives in the Nilgiri Hills. For example:
- During which seasons are crops planted and harvested?
- During which seasons would you need an umbrella? (To provide protection from either the rain or the sun.)
- During which season would it be too wet to hold outdoor meetings?
- What differences are there between the climate in India and in Britain?

- Ask the pupils to draw scenes which illustrate each of the three Indian seasons and the four British seasons. They could write a weather report for a day chosen from each season.

- Pupils could use a thermometer and rain-gauge to record the temperature and rainfall over a week in their local area. TV/radio weather reports, newspaper weather charts and climate data maps in atlases provide further sources of information.

Name:

R10 Climate in the Nilgiri Hills

Use the information about temperature and rainfall in Bangalore to fill in the climate charts on this sheet. Complete the bar chart for rainfall and the line graph for temperature. (Some of the information has already been put in to help you begin.)

On your graphs label the three seasons of the monsoon.

- Cool season: November to March
- Hot season: April to May
- Monsoon season: June to October

Average monthly temperatures in Bangalore

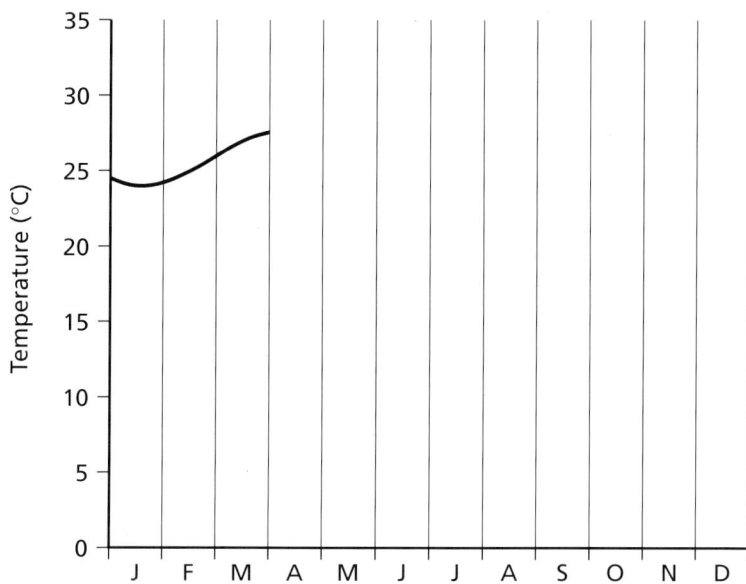

Average temperature (°C)	
J	24
F	25
M	27
A	28
M	30
J	29
J	28
A	27
S	27
O	28
N	27
D	25

Average monthly rainfall in Bangalore

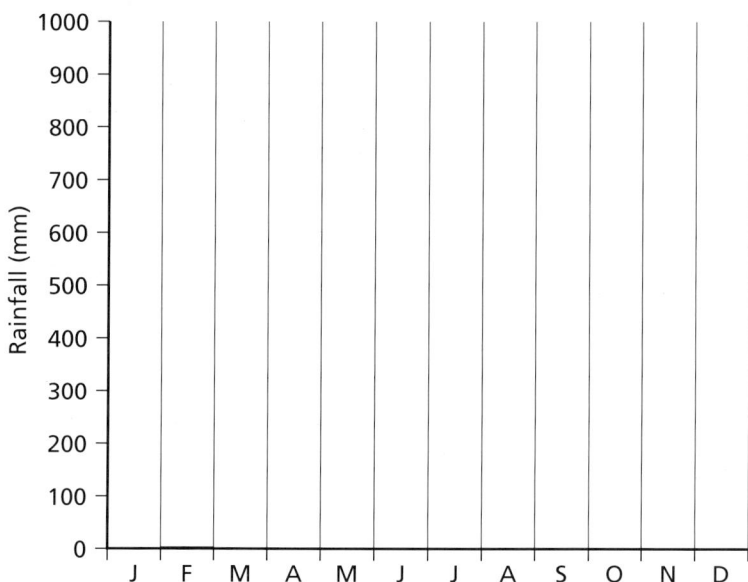

Average rainfall (mm)	
J	0
F	1
M	0
A	0
M	20
J	647
J	945
A	660
S	309
O	117
N	7
D	1

Name:

Climate in London

R11

Using the rainfall and temperature figures for London, complete these two graphs. Draw a bar chart for rainfall and a line graph for temperature. (Again, some of the information has been put in to help you begin.)

- Compare the seasons in London to those in Bangalore.
- What differences can you see between the temperature in these two places?
- When does most rain fall in Bangalore?
- Which months are wet in London?

Average monthly temperatures in London

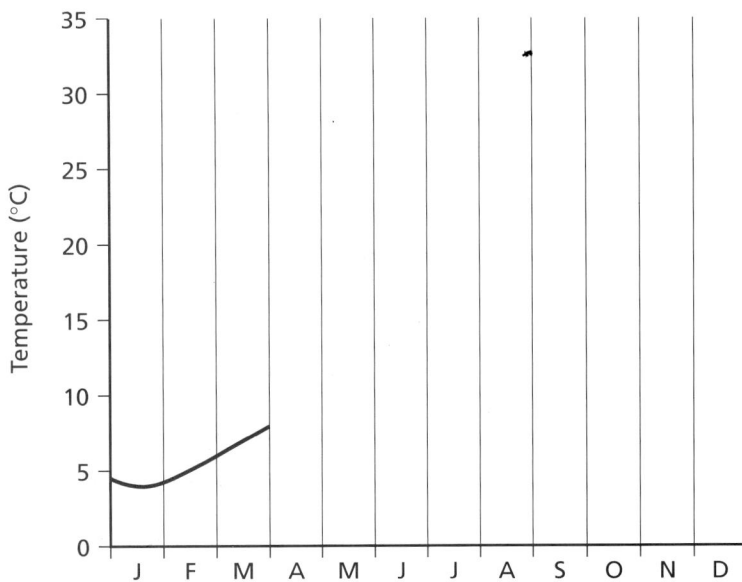

Average temperature (°C)	
J	4
F	5
M	7
A	9
M	12
J	16
J	18
A	17
S	15
O	11
N	8
D	5

Average monthly rainfall in London

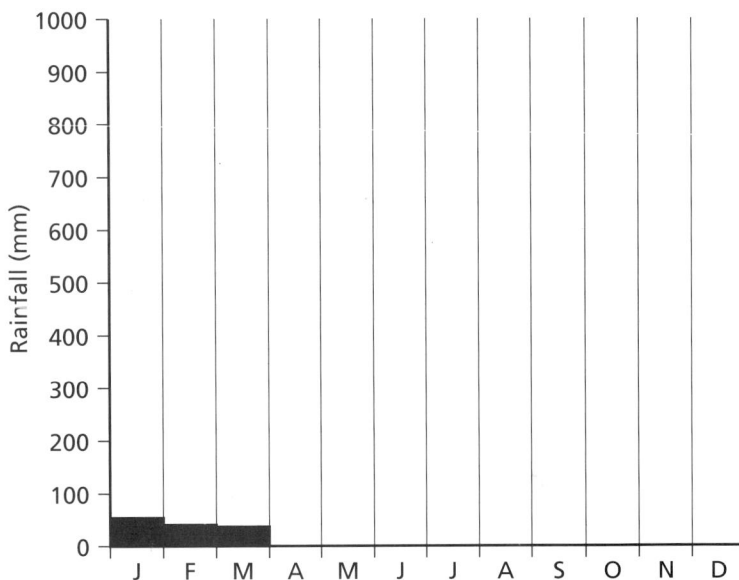

Average rainfall (mm)	
J	54
F	40
M	37
A	37
M	46
J	45
J	57
A	59
S	49
O	57
N	64
D	48

Life in the Nilgiri Hills

The Adivasis

One group of people living in the Nilgiri Hills are Adivasis. Adivasi is the collective name given to India's tribal people. There are 50 million Adivasis in India, made up of 100 tribes speaking over 200 languages. The Adivasis are distributed across India, 95% of them living in rural places, particularly in highland areas such as the Nilgiri Hills. Their ancestors were some of the earliest inhabitants in these areas – there have been Adivasi people living in the Nilgiri Hills since the second century BC.

Some Adivasi people are Hindus and some are Christians. Other Adivasis worship their own gods. The Adivasi people living in the Nilgiri Hills pray to the spirits of the world around them: the trees, the sky, the animals, the earth itself.

While Adivasis are not part of the Hindu caste system, they have been traditionally treated as low-caste. Under the Indian constitution the Adivasi people, along with the 'scheduled' or low (untouchable) castes, are granted special help. The state governments are supposed to make special provision for these people such as job protection and development work.

Family life

There are about 50 families living in each of the villages in the Nilgiri Hills area. Families are very reliant on each other. Everyone works long hours to ensure there is enough food and money to provide for their needs. With no unemployment benefit or state pensions in India it is the family which provides for everyone.

The family at the heart of the locality study in *Village life in India* is introduced on page 12 of the Pupil's Book. Their daily life is represented in picture form on pages 16–17 of the Pupil's Book.

RESOURCE SHEET 12

The text given below is a listening test which illustrates aspects of life for the family of Chandran and Padmini. Ask the pupils to listen to the information in the text as you read it out. Next give out Resource Sheet 12 and let the children read the family's statements. Read out the text again and ask the pupils to fill in the correct information on their sheets. The words given in italics in the text below contain the missing information.

There are five people in this family: two adults, Padmini and Chandran, and *three* children – Bintha, Bomman and Ketan. They own half a *hectare* of land, and grow *tea*, *coffee*, *vegetable*s and bananas. To earn money they work for other people. Padmini picks *tea*, sometimes with her *mother*, while Chandran works in the *ginger fields*. Some of their wages are used to send Bintha to *school*. There she has lessons in subjects such as *English*, *Tamil* and *maths*. After school Bintha plays kokko, similar to *musical chairs*. The family are Adivasis, although there are other religions in this area. Some of Bintha's classmates are *Christians* and *Hindus*. To help the local people, Padmini is a *health worker* and Chandran runs a community group called a *sangham*. These groups help to *protect* the Adivasi's land.

RESOURCE SHEET 13

Pupils should identify the similarities and differences between their lives and this family's life. Resource Sheet 13 shows Bintha's school timetable and a timeline of the family's history. Using this information pupils could draw up similar timelines for their own lives.

Name:

R12 Family life listening test

Chandran says:

We don't own very much land, our field is only about half
a _ _ _ _ _ _ _ _ .
On this land I grow _ _ _ , _ _ _ _ _ _ _
_ _ _ _ _ _ _ _ _ _ and bananas.
To earn money I work in the _ _ _ _ _ _
_ _ _ _ _ _ .
I help run a community group – a _ _ _ _ _ _ _ _ . This
group helps to _ _ _ _ _ _ _ the land owned by the
Adivasi people.

Padmini says:

I am a _ _ _ _ _ _ _   _ _ _ _ _ _ in Kanjikolly
village.
I also earn 25 rupees a day from picking _ _ _ .
My _ _ _ _ _ _ also picks tea.
I have _ _ _ _ _ children: Bintha, Bomman and Ketan.

Bintha says:

Most of my classmates are Adivasis, although others are
_ _ _ _ _ _ _ _ _ _ _ or _ _ _ _ _ _ _ . My
parents use some of the money they earn to send me to
_ _ _ _ _ _ . After school I play kokko which is a
game like _ _ _ _ _ _ _   _ _ _ _ _ _ _ .
At school I have lessons such as _ _ _ _ _ _ _ ,
_ _ _ _ _ and _ _ _ _ _ _ .

R13 Timetables and timelines

Bintha's school day at Kallichal school

8.30 a.m.	9.00 a.m.	9.30 a.m.	10.00 a.m.	10.30 a.m.	11.00 a.m.	11.30 a.m.
Breakfast		Assembly	Registration, Lesson 1 – Mathematics		Lesson 2 – Tamil	Break

12.00 noon	12.30 p.m.	1.00 p.m.	1.30 p.m.	2.00 p.m.	2.30 p.m.	3.00 p.m.
Lesson 3 – Mathematics		Lunch		Lesson 4 – English		Break

3.30 p.m.	4.00 p.m.	4.30 p.m.	5.00 p.m.	5.30 p.m.	6.00 p.m.	6.30 p.m.
Lesson 5 – Citizenship		Finish school		Dinner and free time		

- Compare your school day to Bintha's. What is the same and what is different?

Family history timeline

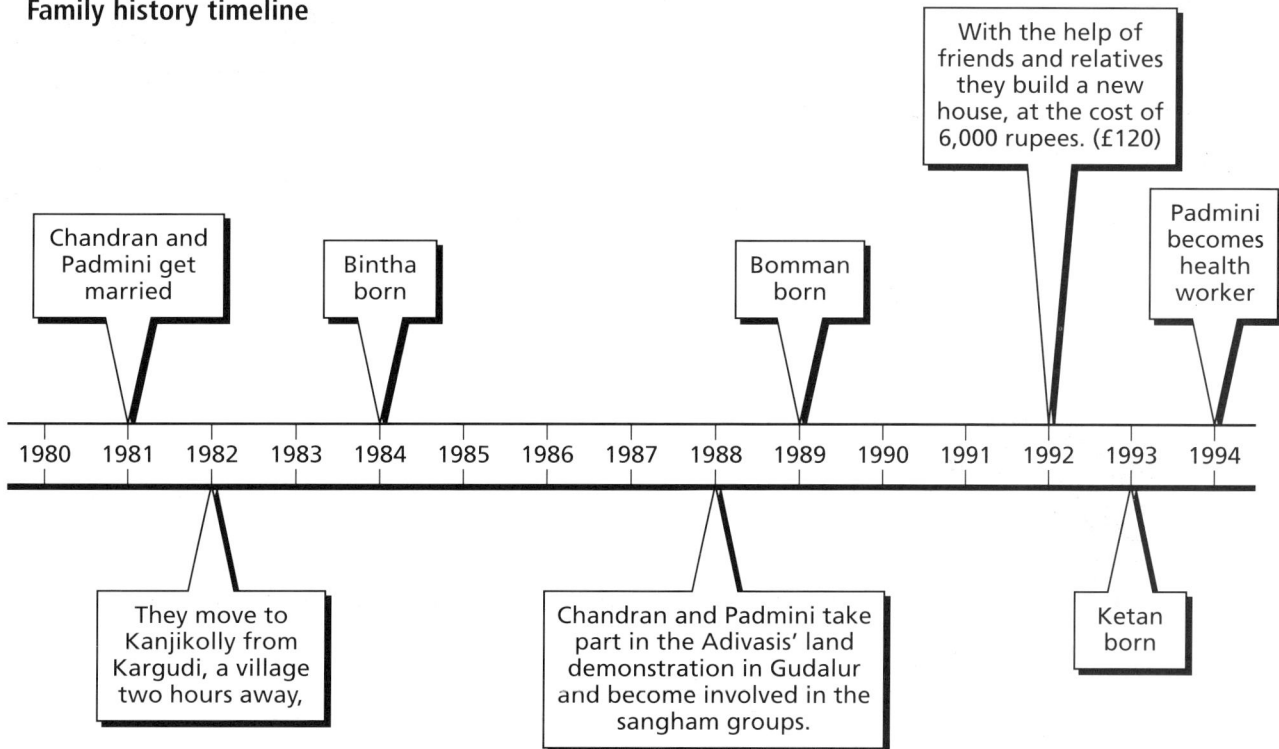

With the help of friends and relatives they build a new house, at the cost of 6,000 rupees. (£120)

Padmini becomes health worker

Chandran and Padmini get married

Bintha born

Bomman born

1980 1981 1982 1983 1984 1985 1986 1987 1988 1989 1990 1991 1992 1993 1994

They move to Kanjikolly from Kargudi, a village two hours away,

Chandran and Padmini take part in the Adivasis' land demonstration in Gudalur and become involved in the sangham groups.

Ketan born

- Make a timeline for your family or yourself.

Water

In India only 57 per cent of the population have safe drinking water and 10 per cent have access to proper sanitation. In this area, one of the jobs which has to be done every day without fail is to collect water. There is no running water in Chembakolli, and people have to collect all the water needed for drinking and cooking from local wells and springs. It is the women and girls of the family who have to collect the water, typically carrying containers which hold over 6 litres of water. This is very heavy and tiring work, and women can spend many hours making sure there is enough water for everyone in the family. Women often have to make two trips per day to collect enough water for the family's daily requirements. A round trip to the well may take up to an hour.

Many of the sources of water people use are 'unprotected'. This means they are also used as watering holes for animals. This can lead to the sources becoming polluted. Health problems linked to dirty water include parasites, dysentery and cholera. Health workers like Padmini place a great deal of emphasis on hygiene education.

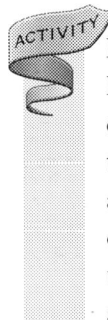

ACTIVITY

In the UK, diarrhoea is not serious but in India, where health services are limited, it can kill children. One successful method of treatment is very simple: children in India are given a salt and sugar solution. Pupils can make up this solution in the classroom using half a litre of water, a teaspoon of sugar and a pinch of salt.

To improve the quality of the water in this area, ACTIONAID funded an Indian charity which helped the local Adivasi people to dig wells and set up pumps. Once a well has been dug, the top is sealed with concrete to prevent animals polluting the water and a pump is installed. The pumps are also a good place for people to meet and talk with friends.

RESOURCE SHEET 14

Resource sheet 14 introduces pupils to the water cycle. There is a section on the water cycle included in the *Village life in India* CD-Rom. This section also includes an interactive graphic display of the climate information for London and Bangalore.

How much water do you use?

Make a list of the different ways you use water during the day. Use the following table to survey your family's use of water.

- How much water does your family use in a day?
- Can you suggest any ways in which you could cut down on the water you use?
- Where would you get water if the supplies to your homes were cut off?
- Which water sources are safe to drink in the UK?

Flushing the toilet	10 litres
One bath	80 litres
One shower	20 litres
One washing machine	100 litres
Dishwasher	50 litres
Washing up in a bowl	15 litres

Name:

Where does water come from?

This diagram shows a section of land and sea. You can
see what happens in the water cycle.

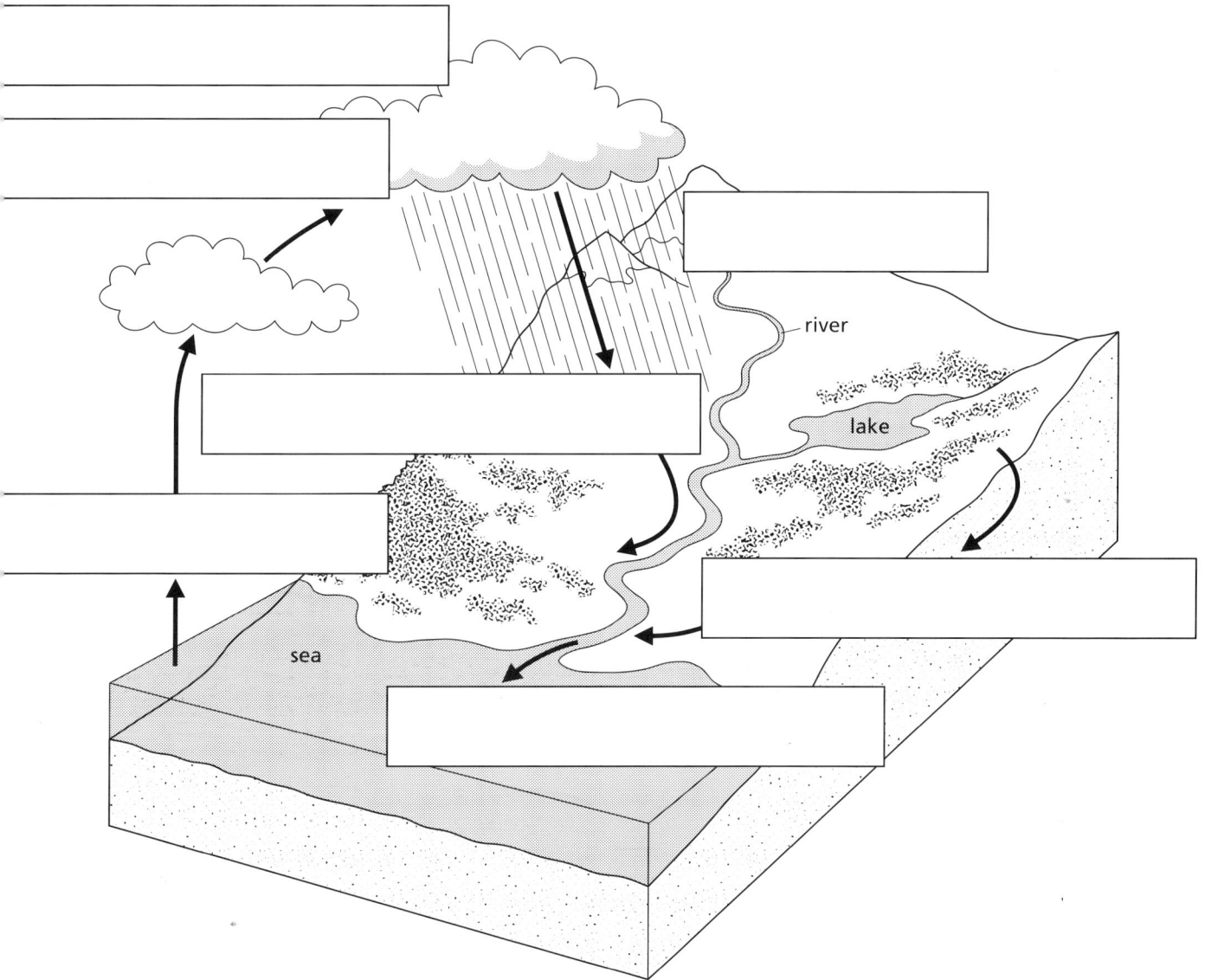

river

lake

sea

- Fill in the boxes on the diagram to explain what is
  happening. Use the list in the Water Cycle box to
  help you.
- The word 'cycle' means circle. Explain why this is
  called the 'water cycle'.

The Water Cycle

Water evaporates from sea

Water vapour forms clouds

Clouds blow over land

Rainfall

Water forms rivers and
drains into ground

Ground water drains into
rivers

Rivers run into sea

ACTIONAID

Farming in the Nilgiri Hills

Farming is very important in this area. Most people rely on agriculture for their livelihood. The farming year is closely linked to the cycle of the monsoon. Just before the monsoon rains start in June, the fields are cleared and the seeds planted. Over the next few months the monsoon rains water the crops. While the crops are growing, between September and December, the fields have to be weeded. Finally, after the crops have ripened, they are harvested during December, January and February.

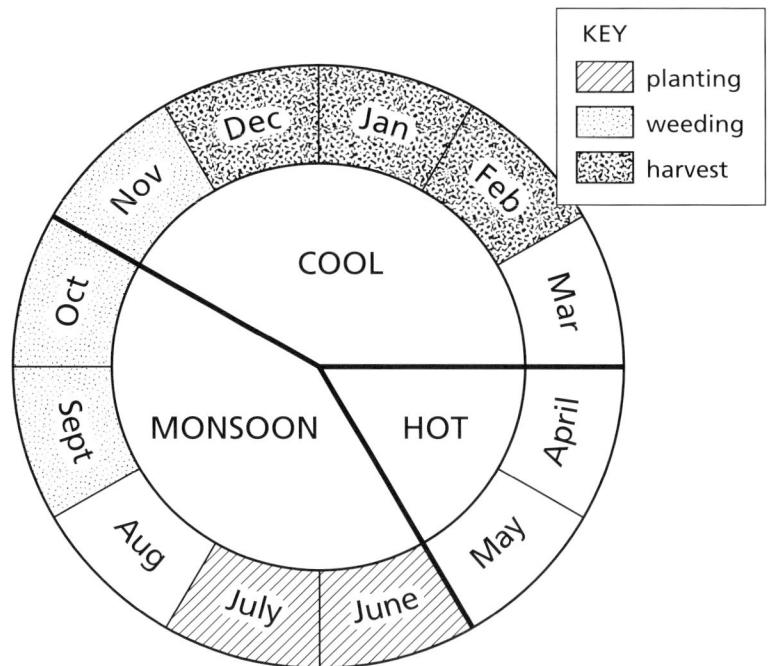

KEY

⬚ planting

⬚ weeding

⬚ harvest

The Adivasis own relatively small plots of land, often not much more than one hectare in size. On this land they grow 'food crops', including rice, bananas, tomatoes, onions, okra and other vegetables. These are crops which will be eaten by the family themselves.

The richer farmers, who are not Adivasis, own larger fields. They mainly grow 'cash crops', such as ginger, tea and coffee. These are crops which will be sold at the local markets to earn the farmer money.

The Adivasis tend not to grow cash crops. This is because they do not have enough money for the seeds, or for agricultural inputs such as pesticides and fertilisers. In order to earn money, the Adivasis work on the fields of the rich farmers. Jobs include picking tea, clearing the land and harvesting ginger. The problem for the Adivasis is that farming work is only available during certain months of the year.

Animals are also kept. Rich farmers might keep a number of pigs and cows. Amongst the Adivasis, the animals are looked after by the women and children. They can usually only afford to keep one cow, a goat and maybe a few chickens. Elephants are used to help with the forestry work such as carrying timber. The elephants are looked after by keepers, known as 'mehabs'. Each mehab is paid 1,400 rupees a month (about £28.00) by the Forestry Department for their work.

Sometimes the men of the village hunt for small animals in the forest. They hunt wild boar, porcupines, deer and rabbits but, because large areas of the forest have been cleared for farmland the amount of wildlife has been reduced.

The forest also provides honey, for those brave enough to collect it, from the nests of wild bees. To make the bees drowsy, the honey collectors blow smoke into the bees' nest. The honeycomb can then be lifted out safely. This can be risky work, particularly for people like Chandran who is allergic to bee stings!

ACTIVITY Ask the pupils to investigate the topic of honey and bee-keeping.

- In which other countries or historical times have bees been kept? What different types of honey can the pupils collect?
- What do the honey-jar wrappers tell you about where the honey is from and the type of plants used by the bees to make it?

ACTIVITY Ask the pupils to use reference books and encyclopaedias to find out more about the lives of elephants.

- In which other countries do elephants live?
- What are the differences between Indian and African elephants?

Pupils could also investigate the other types of animals which live in India.

- Ask the pupils to make a list of the different ways they use animals and animal products. Compare this list to how animals are used in India.

Tea

India is the world's largest producer and exporter of tea. Over 98 per cent of India's tea is grown in the four states of Assam, Bengal, Kerala and Tamil Nadu. Almost 60 per cent of the tea grown in India is drunk within the country itself; the remainder is exported. The largest markets for India's tea are Britain, Russia, Egypt, Iran and Iraq.

Tea statistics (1989)	
World total production of tea	2,460,000 tonnes
Indian production of tea	680,000 tonnes
Indian export of tea	220,000 tonnes
Value of Indian tea exports	£327 million

Tea was first introduced into the Nilgiri Hills by the British colonists during the nineteenth century. This area was climatically suitable for this crop. The huge tea plantations provided a cheap source of tea which could be exported back to Britain's markets.

The plantations were originally owned by European companies. Today one of the few opportunities the Adivasis have of earning money is by working as tea pickers.

The tea bushes need picking every 15 days. One day's work, picking about 25 kg of tea leaves, would earn a woman tea picker 25 rupees (50 pence). Recently an ACTIONAID tea nursery has supplied free tea seedlings to the Adivasis. This has allowed them to earn money from growing their own tea.

RESOURCE SHEET 15

Resource sheet 15 traces the journey of tea, from the tea bush to the teapot. Copy the sheet and cut out the nine cards. Ask the pupils to arrange the cards in the correct order. Can the pupils identify any other stages in the journey? The children could then mount the pictures in the correct order and write labels under each stage, explaining what is happening.

ACTIVITY

- In the Nilgiri Hills tea is whisked up to make it sweet and frothy. Ask the pupils to make a list of the different ways tea can be drunk (e.g. with lemon) and different flavours of tea.
- Ask the pupils to collect different packets of tea. What information can they find on the packs which tells them where the tea came from?
- Nilgiri Hill Blue Mountain Earl Grey Fairtrade Tea is available from major supermarkets. For more information contact The Fairtrade Foundation (see resource list on page 48).

Name:

R15 # What goes into making a cup of tea?

ACTIONAID

Journeys in the Nilgiri Hills

Most journeys in the Nilgiri Hills are on foot. They take place in the local area and are made for different reasons such as:

- going to work: to the family's fields, tea plantations or ginger fields;
- collecting resources for the family: water, fuelwood or hunting animals;
- social reasons: attending sanghams, religious festivals, or meeting friends and relatives;
- visiting the village shops or tea shops;
- going to school or the health centre.

There are also journeys made outside the villages. These are usually to gain access to goods and services which are not provided locally. Many people pay 2.5 rupees and take the bus to Gudalur. Here a wide range of goods is available, such as clothing, electrical products and household goods. In Gudalur there are also cinemas, a hospital which treats only Adivasi people, legal centres and government offices which are important in relation to land rights.

There are also people who make visits to this area, including:

- the doctors who make their rounds by jeep;
- a morning collection of milk by a local dairy;
- lorries from the tea-drying factory which collect the harvested tea twice a week;
- ginger collections during the months of December and January;
- a daily ice cream seller who carries a cool-box on his bicycle;
- a newspaper seller who visits in the afternoon.

RESOURCE SHEET 16

These journeys can be compared with those made in the pupils' home locality using Resource Sheet 16.

Additional ways of examining journeys include:

- making mobility maps such as the example below, which show where people travel to;
- measuring their frequency: daily, weekly or monthly;
- using maps to calculate how far people travel;
- analysing who makes the journey, for example: women collecting water or men hunting;
- working out the type of link, for example: leisure, social or economic;
- following the journey of a product such as tea.

Pupils could be asked to use the map of Chembakolli to plan a route with five 'stops'. Then they could write a story of the route describing the different scenes along the way.

Mobility map

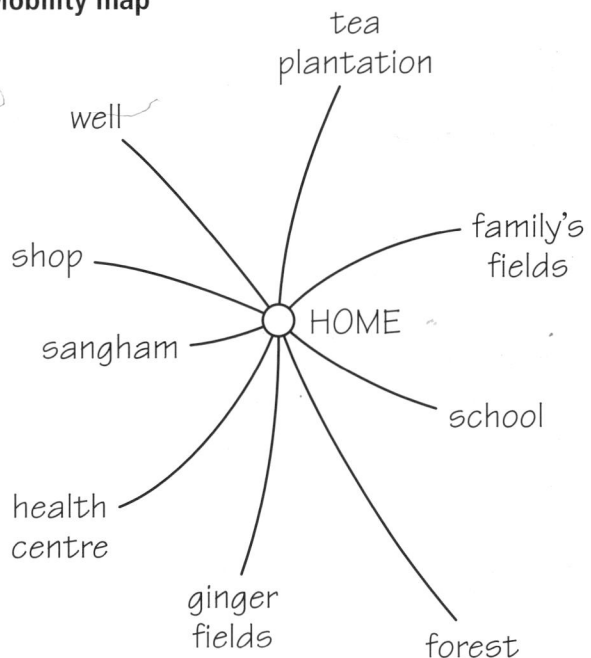

Mobility map showing journeys radiating from HOME to: tea plantation, well, shop, sangham, health centre, ginger fields, forest, school, family's fields.

| **Name:**

R16 Journeys in the Nilgiri Hills and at home

Which places do people visit? Complete the following table.

Where do people go for...	in the Nilgiri Hills	in your local area
food		
water		
wood		
entertainments		
clothing		
household goods		
health care		
education		
to meet other people		

Change and development

Historical change in the Nilgiri Hills

RESOURCE SHEET 17

There have been many historical changes which have affected the land-use of the Nilgiri Hills. The timeline on Resource Sheet 17 provides information on some of these changes. Copy the resource sheet and cut up each sheet to form cards. First ask the pupils, in pairs, to arrange the cards in the correct chronological order. Then ask them to use the information on the cards to identify what changes have occurred in this area. They could use the following headings to categorise the type of change:

- changes to the landscape
- new groups of people moving into the area
- changes in the type of land use
- changes in the types of crops grown

Changes today in the Nilgiri Hills

There are many changes currently occurring in the Nilgiri Hills and it is important for pupils to identify evidence to show these different changes.

RESOURCE SHEET 18

Pupils can complete this work using the 'before and after' approach and Resource Sheet 18. This breaks down the changes into the different themes of:

- landscape
- housing
- farming
- education
- health
- improvements in people's lives
- people's rights to the land

ACTIVITY

Pupils could design their own games on the theme of change, such as:

- **dominoes**
Pupils identify different changes expressed in pairs such as traditional houses and new houses or forested hills matched up to land cleared for fields. Pupils then make dominoes such as those shown on the right using words or sketches of these changes and then play the game by matching the correct 'before' and 'after' pictures.

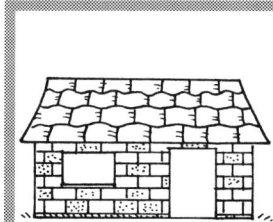

- **snakes and ladders**
A traditional snakes and ladders board is drawn or adapted; the explanation next to each snake or ladder relates to change – a positive change leads to going up and a negative change to going down.

Land rights

One major change in this area was signalled by the Adivasi land rights demonstration. On 5 December 1988 over 10,000 Adivasis demonstrated peacefully in the centre of Gudalur. Because people thought that the Adivasis were disorganised they were expecting only about 30 people to march. On seeing the demonstration stretching for over a mile, the police in Gudalur fled the town, but there was no trouble and the demonstration was well-organised. It had become clear that the Adivasis were going to assert their rights to their land.

Pupils could draw future change lines such as the example shown below, either positive or negative. The aim with future change lines is for the pupils to project into the future different changes which could take place in the Nilgiri Hills. For example, people protect their rights to the land; they are able to plant and sell more tea and, therefore, earn more money. Conversely, a poor harvest or being deprived of their land rights leads to poverty and inability to improve their future.

The Pupil's Book suggests that pupils could produce a radio report describing these events. They could also record the issue from other points of view by writing a diary entry for one of the following people:
- an Adivasi person taking part in the demonstration
- a charity worker who helped to organise the demonstration
- the local police
- a rich farmer who is worried that the Adivasis may claim some of his land.

Use the following questions and prompts for this work:
- What sights would you have seen?
- What would your feelings about the demonstration have been?
- Which side of the demonstration would you have been supporting?
- What might have been your thoughts for the future after the demonstration?

Pupils could then compare their different accounts.

Future change line

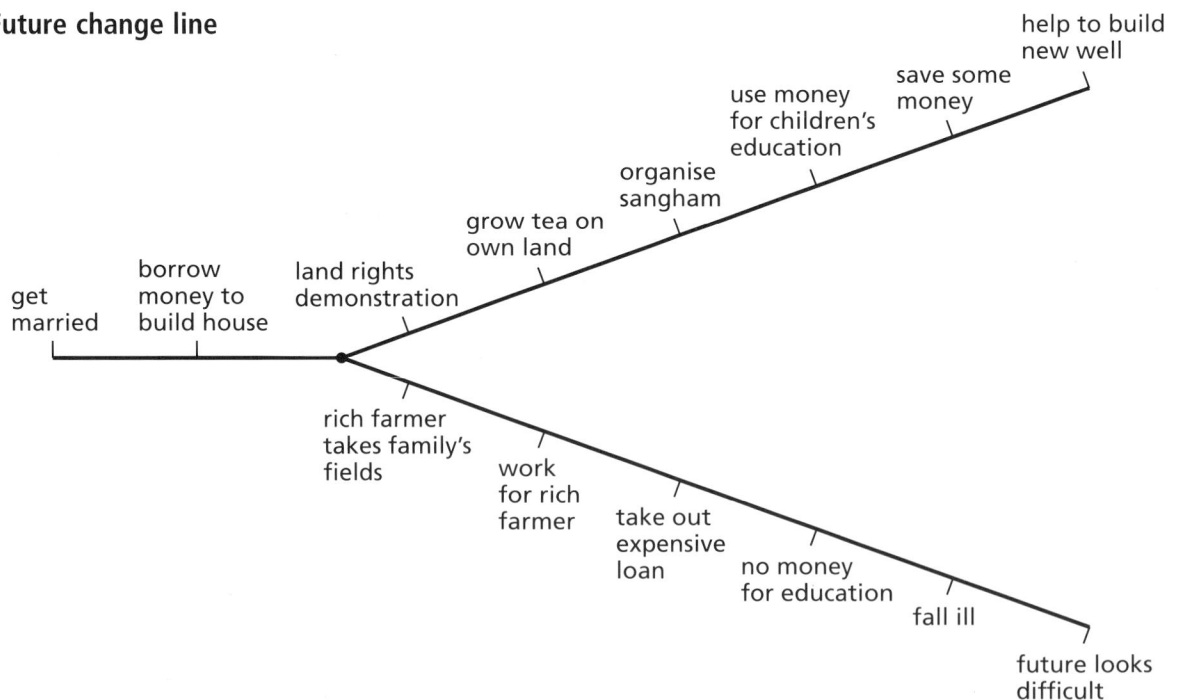

Name:

R17 # How has life changed in the Nilgiri Hills?

During the 8th century there was forest growing on almost all of the Nilgiri Hills and the Adivasi people lived there. They gathered food from the forest and cleared small areas for their fields. They used each field for just one year. Then the Adivasis would move to a new area, and the forest could grow again.

During the 15th century a new type of farming started in this area. It was called 'settled farming'. The forest was cleared and the same field was used year after year.

During the early 19th century the colonists from Britain brought new crops of tea and coffee. Some of the forest was cleared to make space for large tea and coffee plantations. There were about 3,000 people living in this area.

By 1850 the population had grown to nearly 20,000 people. Most of them came from other parts of India looking for farmland and jobs. In 1850 over half of the population was made up of people who had come from other parts of India.

During the 1940s more forest was cleared for farmland. Over half of the farmland was now covered by tea and coffee plantations. The plantations were owned by European companies.

During the 1950s, people were beginning to control malaria – a deadly disease. They were also able to use water power to make electricity. This made the area safer to live in and provided more jobs. Even more people moved into the Nilgiri Hills.

By 1951 farmland covered 45,000 hectares of the Nilgiri Hills – about a fifth of the total area. The population had grown to 300,000 people.

People have continued to move into the Nilgiri Hills. In 1991 704,000 people were living in the Nilgiri Hills; 80 per cent of them were originally from outside this area. Nearly 30 per cent of the forest has been cleared for farmland.

ACTIONAID

Name:

R18 What changes are occurring in the Nilgiri Hills?

This table shows some of the changes which are
taking place in the Nilgiri Hills. Use the information
you have found out about life in this area to complete
the gaps.

Change	Before	After
landscape	forested hills	
housing		new types of houses
farming		
education		
health		
land rights	Adivasis driven off their land	

Development

India is not just a country populated by poor people. It has areas of great wealth and in fact, in absolute numbers, there are more middle-class people in India than there are in Britain. However, many millions of people do live in poverty. The case study of the Nilgiri Hills shows how poverty affects people's lives. However, as pupils will have found out, the lack of certain facilities does not mean people in this area are not working to improve their future.

Development relates to the way in which people improve the quality of their lives both economically – through having more money and resources, and socially – through improved health and educational standards. People also need the skill and ability to maintain the improvements they achieve in the future. There are many ways of measuring development. The table given below provides different measures, all of which can be used to examine people's quality of life. The figures can be used to draw different graphs and to compare life in India and Britain.

In the first development project in this area ACTIONAID set up local community groups called sanghams, where people can meet to discuss their needs and plan future improvements. Pupils will find out about the work of the sanghams in chapter 8 of the Pupil's Book.

RESOURCE SHEET
19

The sangham community groups identified the Adivasi people's priorities in the Nilgiri Hills as:
- land rights;
- clean water;
- improved education;
- health care;
- village banks, access to savings and credit;
- new sources of income.

Resource Sheet 19 gives pupils the opportunity to understand how the Adivasis, working together, are beginning to identify and overcome their problems. The resource sheet provides perspectives on these issues from six people in the Nilgiri Hills. Divide the class into groups of six. Tell them to imagine that they live in an Indian village where they face the sort of problems seen in chapter 7 of the Pupil's Book. As a sangham group, they now have to decide what development work they are going to set up. Cut up the resource sheet into six cards. Give the pupils one card each. Ask them to:
- read their card;
- identify what improvements they want and how this will improve life in this area;
- plan a one-minute speech to the rest of the sangham;
- take it in turns to read out their speeches to each other;
- decide, as a group, which are the most important things and then decide what the group could do to improve life in this area;
- compare the outcomes of different groups.

Measuring wealth: India and the UK		
	India	UK
Average amount of wealth per person	£221	£8320
Life expectancy	60 years	75 years
The number of people per doctor	2,400	800
Adults who can read and write	43%	99%
People with safe drinking water	57%	100%
TVs per 1000 people	32	435

Name:

R19 Development

Chandran says:

The forest provides us with food, land and firewood. We must work together to protect our rights to use the forest.

Chanda says:

I collect water every day from the spring. This takes a lot of my time. The spring is also used by animals. We need a clean well which is near to the village.

Penchi says:

There is no school here, so our children must go to the government schools. They teach in a different language. Some teachers look down on Adivasis.

Sumitra says:

I am paying back an expensive loan to a rich farmer. As a result my family is going short of food. If I had a cheap loan I could pay off my debts and buy a sack of rice.

Kelu says:

One of my five children has already died of measles. I know measles can be treated, but in these villages there are no health services.

Karunakan says:

If we could grow tea we could earn more money. Then we would not have to rely on the wages from working for the rich farmers. All we need are some tea seedlings.

Life in India's towns and cities

The growth of cities

Although 77 per cent of the people in India live in the countryside, the size of India's cities has grown rapidly over the last 50 years. By 1990 there were 23 Indian cities which had a population of over 1 million people. This pattern of growth can be seen in the following figures for Bangalore:

The growth of Bangalore	
Date	Population of Bangalore
1941	400,000
1951	800,000
1961	1,200,000
1971	1,700,000
1981	2,900,000
1991	4,100,000

- Ask the pupils to use these figures to draw a bar graph to show the increase in Bangalore's population. What reasons can they suggest for the growth in a city's population?

Bangalore has grown for two reasons:
- people in the city having children;
- more people migrating into the city.

In Bangalore, migration into the city is very important and almost 40 per cent of the people living in the city are migrants. There are many reasons why people move to the city. Amongst male migrants, 50 per cent moved to Bangalore in order to get a better job. The opportunity to get better education and health services is also important. Amongst female migrants one of the important reasons for migration is family obligations – moving to city to be with their husband after marriage, for example.

- Ask the pupils to make a list of the reasons why people might leave the countryside and move to a city.

RESOURCE SHEET 20

The reasons why people migrate can be analysed in two ways:
- push factors: features which force people to move away from the countryside, such as rural poverty, a lack of services or a bad harvest;
- pull factors: features which draw people into the city, such as better jobs, 'the bright lights' or better housing.

Resource Sheet 20 asks pupils to examine the reasons different people living in the Nilgiri Hills give for moving and then to categorise them into push or pull factors.

When people move into a city this increases the need for more housing, jobs, electricity, water and sewage supplies and services. It can be difficult for cities to cope with all the new people. This has occurred in Bangalore where over 400,000 people live in the city's slum areas. For more information on life in India's cities see the *Bangalore, Indian City Life* photopack, for details see the resources list, page 48.

| **Name:**

The growth of cities

The reasons why people move to the city can be called 'push' factors and 'pull' factors:

- **push** factors, for example poverty, a lack of local services or a bad harvest, force people to move away from the countryside;
- **pull** factors, for example better jobs, 'the bright lights' or better housing, attract people into the city.

Read the following quotes from people. Decide whether their reason for moving to the city is a push or a pull factor, and place a cross in the correct box. The first example has been done for you.

	push factor	pull factor		push factor	pull factor
Ravi (man): My cousin lives in the centre of Bangalore and he told me that there is work available there.		X	Mari (woman): My husband-to-be lives in the city. When I get married to him I will go there to live with him.		
Urmil (woman): The nearest doctor is 30 kms away from my village – a long way to walk when you're ill.			Suresh (man): Where I live in the slums, it's hard to get a job. One day I'll leave to try and find regular well-paid work.		
Kelu (woman): Last month the landlord put up the rent on my fields. It's getting too expensive to be a farmer.			Rukku (woman): This year the monsoon failed and my crops didn't grow.		
Sampangi (man): In Madras there are better schools for my children.			Geetha (woman): There are new houses in the city. Some have running water and electricity.		

Differences in India's cities

Despite the poverty of the Chembakolli area, pupils often gain a very positive impression of this locality. With its lush vegetation it often seems a far more interesting and exotic place than it really is when compared to urban environments. Pupils should be able to make more informed comparisons between urban and rural life.

Ask the pupils to list the good and bad points about living in a town and in a village. They should do this in a British and an Indian context, and also from their own and an adult's perspective.

The following information provides some comparative figures for India:

Facilities	urban	rural
number of households	29 million	94 million
houses with electricity	53%	7%
houses with tap water	70%	9%
total wealth per household	£203	£180

What can you find in the city of Bangalore?

Bangalore is one of India's largest cities. It is the nearest city to the case study area of Chembakolli. If you visited any Indian city you would find similar features to those found in Britain including shopping centres, parks, hotels, restaurants, busy roads, different types of housing and factories. However, there would also be street sellers, slum areas, auto-rickshaws, street-children, temples and ox carts.

- Ask the pupils to make a list of five features they would expect to find in a British city. e.g. different types of houses, shops or cinemas. Would they expect to find any of these features in a city in India?

RESOURCE SHEET 21

Resource sheet 21 provides a land-use map for Bangalore. Pupils should first shade over the key in different colours to make the different features stand out. Next ask them to use the information on the key to correctly match up the seven labels to the correct parts of the city. They can then colour the map in accordance with the key.

RESOURCE SHEET 22

Pupils should also recognise that there are differences within towns and cities. Resource sheet 22 allows pupils to analyse two different sides of life in Bangalore.

Make two sets of Resource sheet 22. For the first set blank-off the right hand half of the sheet and for the second blank-off the left hand half. Give different groups of pupils the different sets. Explain that they have half of a picture from Bangalore and ask them to complete the rest of the picture. When the pupils have completed their pictures reveal the 'complete picture'.

- What are the differences between the two styles of buildings? Who might live in the different buildings? Ask the pupils to write estate agent style details for the two housing types.

Comparisons could be made between land use in the city and land use in Chembakolli by using Resource Sheet 8.

Name:

R21 What can you find in the city of Bangalore?

This map shows how land is used in Bangalore. Use the key to find out how each area is used. Colour the map to make the different areas stand out. Use the following colours:

expensive housing – red

low-cost housing – blue

slums – black

factories – green

shops and offices – yellow

Use the key to work out what sort of areas the arrows are pointing at. Fill in each blank box using this list:

- expensive houses
- low-cost houses
- slum houses
- supermarket
- railway station
- computer factory
- traffic jams

KEY	
F	Factories
S	Slums
L	Low cost housing
E	Expensive housing
O	Shops and offices
≈	Road
—	Railway
■	Station

Name:

Cityscapes

R22

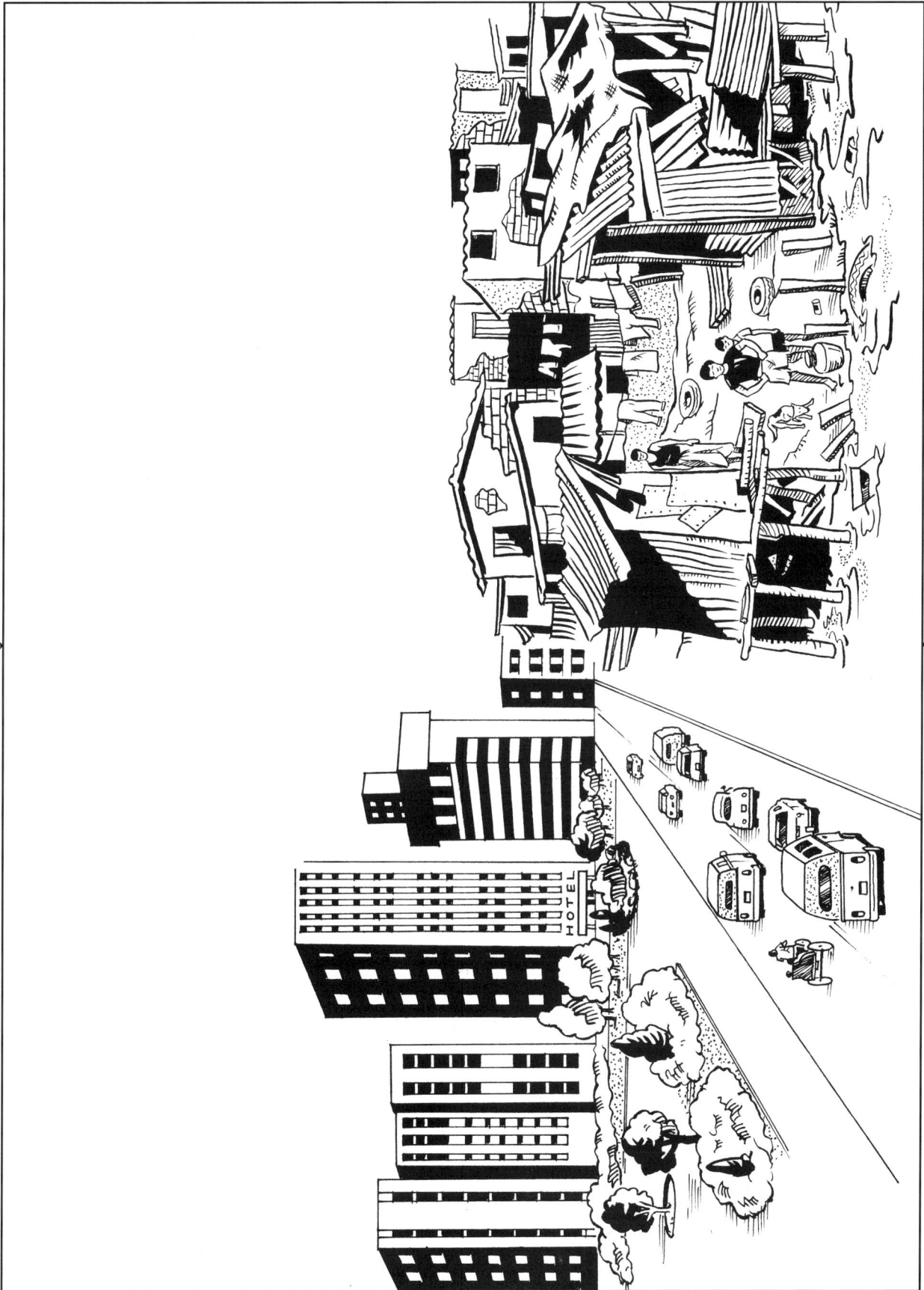

Blank off picture left or right of this line   before photocopying.

Jobs in India

Agriculture is very important to the Indian economy. One third of the people in India rely on agriculture for their livelihood. Other jobs are also important. Since independence from Britain in 1947 India has developed industries such as iron and steel, chemical processing and textiles – and more recently electronic goods, computers and cars. 'White collar' employment has also increased with the expansion of educational and social services, and the growth of business and office jobs.

One way of analysing different jobs is to allocate them to the following categories:

- agricultural: farming, mining and fishing
- manufacturing: factory work and construction
- services: office work, business, finance, social services, education, communications and health.

These three categories are also known as primary, secondary and tertiary industries.

RESOURCE SHEET 23

Copy Resource Sheet 23 and cut it up to form six cards. Ask the pupils to match up the people on the resource cards to the three categories: agricultural
                      manufacturing
                      services
- Ask the pupils to identify the types of job which take place in their local area. Which of them are agricultural, manufacturing or service jobs?

RESOURCE SHEET 24

Using Resource Sheet 24 and the figures given in the table below, ask the pupils to draw two divided bar charts, one for India and a second for Britain. They should shade the key and the columns to show the different categories. An outline is provided on the resource sheet.

Employment statistics		
	India	Britain
agriculture	63%	2%
manufacturing	10%	20%
services	27%	78%

- Ask the pupils to answer the following questions:

Which country has the largest percentage of people employed in agriculture?

Which country has the smallest percentage of people employed in services?

Which country has the largest percentage of people employed in factories?

Is the percentage of people employed in manufacturing in Britain twice or half as many as are found in India?

Why do you think there are more people employed in agriculture in India?

Why do you think there are more people employed in services in Britain?

Name:

R23 | # Jobs in India

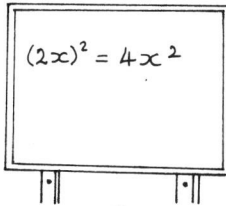

Ravi

I am a maths teacher in a secondary school in Delhi.

Geetha

I work in the accounts department of a bank in Madras.

Binu

Every day I launch my boat from the beach in Orissa to catch fish.

I work carrying bricks on a building site in Bangalore.

Sonara

Bijl

Bangalore is a boom town for computers. I work on an assembly line putting together computers.

One day's work picking tea earns me 25 rupees.

Padmini

Name:

R24 What type of job?

The table below shows the percentage of people doing different types of work in India and in Britain.

Employment statistics		
	India	Britain
agriculture	63%	2%
manufacturing	10%	20%
services	27%	78%

In India, 63% of people work in agriculture. Look at the India chart to see how this figure is shown as a column. Now use the other percentage figures to draw columns in both of the charts.

- Use three different colours for the columns in your charts and colour the key to match.

- When you have completed your charts, compare them and see what differences you can find.

KEY

☐ agriculture

☐ manufacturing

☐ services

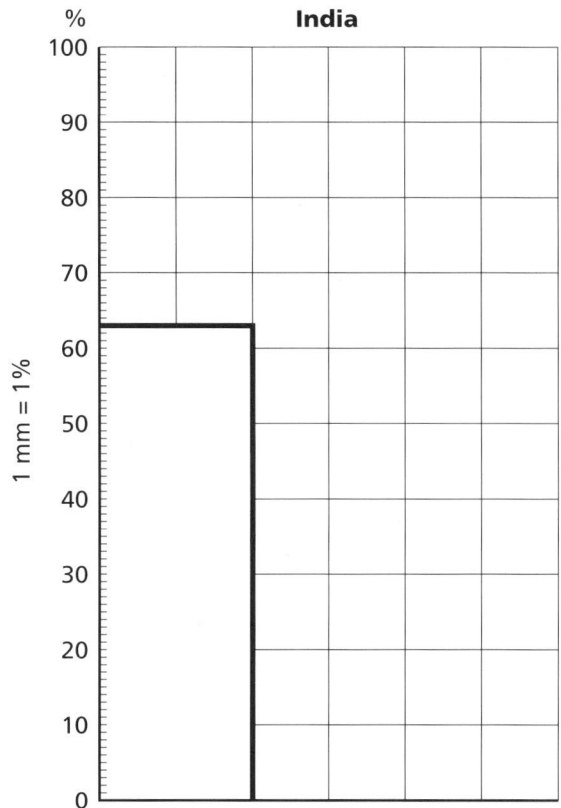

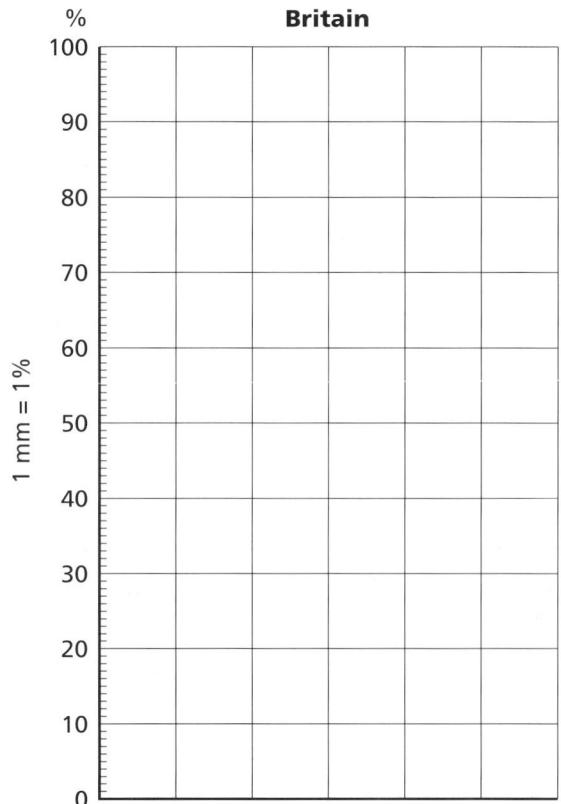

© Cambridge University Press 1996

Travel and tourism

Travelling around India

Roads

There are over 33,000 km of main road in India. Many villages are not linked to the road network, although there are plans to provide a road link to every village with a population of over 1,500 people. However, even when settlements are linked up, road travel can still be very time-consuming. This is shown in the Nilgiri Hills when a journey of 14 km from Kanjikolly to Gudalur takes over an hour because of the poor state of the roads.

Rail

After the USA, Russia and Canada, India – with its 61,000 km of track – has the fourth largest rail network in the world. Railways were introduced to India by the British. The first service was on 31 March 1853 when trains started to run along 34 km of track between Bombay and Thana.

In rural areas the most common forms of transport are by foot, bicycle or bus. By contrast, in the towns and cities, the streets are often full of cars, motorbikes, lorries, auto-rickshaws and also, perhaps rather surpisingly, red London buses.

Air travel

There are four major Indian airports in India: Bombay, Delhi, Calcutta and Madras. The flight time from Britain to India is about eight hours. India is five and a half hours ahead of GMT.

- Pupils could use maps from tourist brochures to identify the flight path from Britain to India. They could then trace the route using a globe. Which countries would the plane fly over? How far is it from Britain to India? How many time zones does the air traveller cross?

Making connections

There are many connections between India and Britain. Some of the links stretch back hundreds of years, while others are more recent.

ACTIVITY Pupils can categorise these links in the following ways:

Trade   Find out what Indian produce is sold in local shops.

Food   Survey the class to see who eats Indian food.

Language   Find the meanings of English words which were derived from India such as bungalow, dinghy, jungle, chutney, shampoo, curry or jodhpurs.

Colonial links   The Commonwealth Institute in London has a permanent display on India.

Sporting links   Polo was imported from Indian to Britain, Conversely cricket, inherited from Britain, is a very popular game in India.

Family links and visits   Some pupils may have family connections with India or have visited this country. They can provide evidence illustrating contrasts across India. A pupil may say: 'I visited my grandparents and where they lived was nothing like Chembakolli', or: 'All I did was lie on a beach in Goa!'

Tourism

Name:

R25 Travelling around India

Madras	Hyderabad	Delhi	Calcutta	Bombay	Bangalore	
704						
2157	1453					
1678	1516	1442				
1367	739	1408	2081			
334	566	2019	1883	1033		
1957	1253	200	1242	1208	1819	Agra

(kilometres)

How to use the mileage table

How far is it from Madras to Agra?
Find Madras and Agra on the table. Follow a straight line down from Madras and another straight line across from Agra. The square where the two lines cross shows the distance between the two places in kilometres – 1957 km.

1 Work out the straight-line distance from:
Hyderabad to Madras;
Bombay to Delhi;
Agra to Bangalore;
Delhi to Calcutta.

2 How far would you travel if you completed these journeys?
Agra to Bangalore to Hyderabad;
Delhi to Hyderabad to Calcutta;
a return trip from Calcutta to Bombay;
a return trip from Madras to Hyderabad via Bangalore.

3 If a train travels at 60 km an hour how long would these journeys take?
Agra to Madras;
Bombay to Calcutta;
Delhi to Madras via Calcutta.

ACTIONAID

Name:

Tourism in India

R26

Goa, a state in India, is a popular tourist location. Here are six interviews with people who live there. Use the information to find out three advantages and three disadvantages of tourism. Then fill in the grid.

Tourists ignore all our customs. If you are a visitor in someone else's country you should behave well!

I work in one of the beach hotels. It's a lot better working here and I make more money than in other jobs.

Tourists spend money which is good for the economy and good for my hotel business.

The hotels need a large water supply so there is less water left for our fields.

Many of the hotels are owned by foreigners so there is less benefit to the Indian people.

The tourists buy my statues. I make a good living.

Advantages	Disadvantages

- Use the following figures to draw a bar graph to show the increase in tourists in Goa. What is happening to the number of tourists in this area?

1972	10,000
1990	1,000,000
2000	5,000,000 (projected)

- How do tourists help India's economy?
- What types of facilities do foreign tourists expect to have when they go on holiday?
- How does tourism affect people's lives in India?

ACTIONAID 47

Resources and useful addresses

ACTIONAID produces an award winning range of materials which build on the work of this series:

Chembakolli, a Village in India   Locality photopack containing 30 A4 colour photographs of scenes from the village, pupil resource sheets, background information booklets and maps.

Kanjikolly, Working Together   Two, 20 minute videos, plus activity sheets, following a day in the life of Kanjikolly village. Explores the family life of Padmini and Chandran and links with the town of Gudalur.

Village life in India   CD-Rom. 9 sections of interactive material including a village study of Kanjikolly, which supports and extends this locality study. Contains video, still pictures, soundtrack, maps, diagrams and exercises. CUP/ACTIONAID

Bangalore, Indian City Life   Locality photopack examining life in Bangalore, particularly through the eyes of a group of street boys. Contains 30 A4 colour photographs, resource sheets, background information booklets and an adventure booklet.

Neighbours, the life of Yesudas Kemal   30 minute video examining family life on the outskirts of Delhi.

Mullavassal   Role-play based on development priorities for a village.

ACTIONAID also provides a school speaker service. For visit details and to order materials contact: Gideon Ellwood, Development Education, ACTIONAID, Chataway House, Leach Road, Chard, Somerset TA20 1FA. Tel: 01460 62972.

The Commonwealth Institute has a permanent display on India. It also provides resources and a school visits service. Commonwealth Institute, 230 Kensington High Street, London W8 6NQ. Tel: 0171 6034535.

The Development Education Association can provide the address of a local resource centre carrying materials on India and other countries. Development Education Association, Third Floor, 29–31 Cowper Street, London EC2A 4AP. Tel: 0171 4908108.

The Fairtrade Foundation, 7th Floor, Regent House, 89 Kingsway, London, WC2B 6RH. Tel: 0171 4055942.

High Commissioner for India, India House, Aldwych, London WC2.

The Oxfam catalogue carries many materials on India and other countries. Oxfam, Development Education, 274 Banbury Road, Oxford, OX2 7DZ. Tel: 01865 312353

Soma Books Ltd, stock books and materials from India. Soma Books, 38 Kennington Land, London SE11 4LS

Tourism Concern Southlands College, Wimbledon Parkside, London SW19 5NN. Tel: 0181 9440464